Cookstown

from Lough Neagh to the Sperrins

Paintings by John S. Haggan

Text by Eddie McCartney

Cottage
Publications

First published by Cottage Publications,
Donaghadee, N. Ireland 1999.
Copyrights Reserved.
© Illustrations by John S. Haggan 1999.
© Text by Eddie McCartney 1999.

Design & origination in Northern Ireland.
Printed & bound in Singapore.

ISBN 1 900935 11 2

The Author

Cookstown born and bred, Eddie McCartney was educated at Cookstown High School. A teacher all his days, he was principal of Coagh Primary School for 21 years until his retirement. Together with Alison Hedger, he has co-written a number of children's musicals, published by Golden Apple Productions, a division of Music Sales Ltd. and he is a member of the British Academy of Composers and Songwriters. A gifted poet, Eddie has twice won awards in the prestigious Patrick MacGill poetry competition, and he has also been runner-up in the 'Bard of Armagh' competition. His work has been published in a number of anthologies and he has been honoured by Cookstown District Council for his outstanding contribution to the Arts in the Cookstown area.

Eddie has a keen interest in local history, chairing both Cookstown History Group, and the editorial committee of the mid-Ulster historical journal, 'Look Back'. He lives in Cookstown with his wife, Martha and has a son, Mark and daughter, Karen.

The Artist

John Haggan worked as an industrial engineer until 1979 when, with the encouragement of his friends, he decided to become a professional artist. His work has now been exhibited in galleries all over Northern Ireland and he has received commissions from as far afield as New Zealand, U.S.A., Canada and South Africa. He also has contracts with Felix Rosentiels, the world's largest Fine Art publisher.

John's style has been compared to that of many 18th and 19th century artists. His landscapes capture the peace and tranquillity of the rivers, streams and valleys of Ulster and often incorporate the rural activities of yesteryear. His work has been the subject of several television programmes and he has had numerous paintings reproduced for calendars and cards.

John now lives in Cookstown where he owns and runs the Gallery One Arts Centre, an outlet for his own work and that of other talented artists (often those he has taught himself).

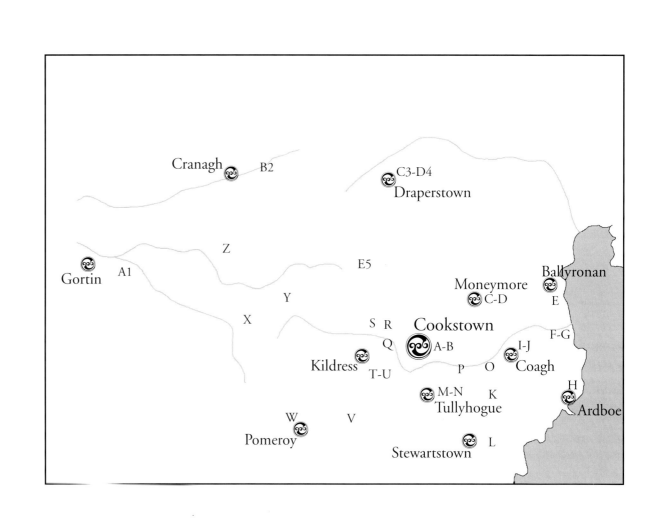

Cranagh ⊚ B2

⊚ C3-D4
Draperstown

Z

E5

⊚ Ballyronan

Gortin ⊚ A1

Moneymore
⊚ C-D   E

Y

X   S R   Cookstown
                          Q   ⊚ A-B   F-G
                                                ⊚ I-J
Kildress ⊚   P   O   Coagh
         T-U   H
                       ⊚ M-N   K   ⊚
                       Tullyhogue   Ardboe

W   V

Pomeroy ⊚

Stewartstown ⊚ L

Contents

Beginnings

The area of mid-Ulster described in this book is centred around Cookstown in Co. Tyrone. A district containing some excellent farming land, it is bounded to the west by the Sperrin Mountains and to the east by Lough Neagh. It stretches beyond Stewartstown to the south and north to Ballyronan on the lough shore.

The gently rolling, heather-clad Sperrins curve round to the north of Cookstown, and Slieve Gallion provides an impressive backdrop to the town. The highest peak in the Sperrins is Mount Sawel. The area is almost bisected by that anglers' paradise, the River Ballinderry. The river meanders peacefully from the west, past the southern end of Cookstown under the King's Bridge, onwards to the village of Coagh and into Lough Neagh, the largest freshwater lake in Ireland and Great Britain.

The undulating nature of this part of mid-Ulster is the result of an extended period of submersion below the sea, combined with the buckling effect of tremendous internal pressure and the effects of successive glacial flows.

The frequent subsidences of the land beneath the sea led to the laying down of sandstone sediments which were pressed down to become rock. The main sandstone found in the area is old red sandstone around the base of Slieve Gallion. When the sea became warmer, due to climatic changes, small sea creatures thrived. As countless millions of these died and sank to the bottom, their remains formed limestone. Coal seams also developed thousands of millions of years ago, formed from dense forests that were pushed down by gigantic pressure from overlying clay.

The later volcanic activity which began in north east Ulster produced basalt flows which reached the mid-Ulster area and served to protect the seams from successive ice flows. This explains why coal was preserved in the area and why workable coal is not found in many other places in Ireland.

Not far from Cookstown, between Tullyhogue and Stewartstown, the small coal deposit at Cratley was worked until just before the last war. Further on from Stewartstown, coal was mined at Coalisland until the early 1960s. The Coalisland coalfields are found within an area of five square miles and are mainly within the boundaries of the Congo fault to the north, the Drumkeen fault to the west and the river Torrent to the west and south. Large quantities of Coalisland coal were extracted over the years and miners often worked under extremely difficult and dangerous conditions.

During the glacial period the north east of Ireland was engulfed by ice from the Firth of Clyde in Scotland. The ice flow continued inexorably to a western limit which included the Sperrin Mountains. It created innumerable drumlins which are long, low, gently rounded hills. The prefix 'drum' is taken from the Irish meaning 'ridge' and the frequency with which this prefix occurs in the names of the townlands that surround Cookstown indicates drumlin country. Some examples are Drum, Drummond, Drumcraw, Drumard, Drumgarrell, Drumearn, Drumraw and Drumballyhugh. The drumlins left by the glaciers contain vast deposits of sand and gravel which have been exploited commercially for many years. There are a great number of sand and gravel pits in the mid-Ulster area which make an invaluable contribution to the building industry.

The glacial flow from Scotland left evidence of its origin in the form of erratics. Erratics are rocks found in an area of which they are not typical so it has to be concluded that they were brought from another location. In the mid-Ulster area are found erratics of Ailsa Craig and Arran granite which the glaciers deposited as they flowed west from Scotland. The lakes in the vicinity of the Sperrin Mountains and Lough Neagh itself are the result of this glacial activity.

If you fancy trying your hand at prospecting for gold, the Sperrin Mountains would be a good place to try your luck. Gold has been obtained from the streams of the Sperrins for centuries, especially near Plumbridge. Be warned, the returns for your efforts will be very small but there is the possibility that you might experience the thrill of discovering some minute specks of the precious metal. Consideration has been given to obtaining gold by large scale commercial operations. Such a venture would, however, have to be weighed against the possible effect on the environment and there is no guarantee that such an operation would be financially viable.

About two miles to the south west of Cookstown is Slieve More, where red garnets have been found.

A few miles to the west of the town, haematite

ore is found at Lissan in the townland of Unagh, though this is no longer extracted. It was used for producing iron and a small foundry was in operation there early in the 17th century using oak, which was then in plentiful supply, as charcoal for smelting the ore. The foundry belonged to the Staples family.

Peat bogs are present in the area and are more prevalent as you move towards the Sperrin Mountains. The majority of this bogland was formed during the period 500 – 100 BC as succeeding layers of peat vegetation and sphagnum moss accumulated. The turf from the bogs has been a useful source of fuel for many generations. The bogland is also a haven for plant and animal life and provides a valuable resource for ecologists.

On the shore of Lough Neagh, near Washing Bay, there are extensive deposits of lignite. Lignite, often called 'brown coal', is the substance which, in layman's terms, is intermediate between turf and coal. However, as this area is an unspoilt haven for plant, animal and bird life, commercial exploitation of the lignite, if it should ever be considered, would have to take careful account of this.

In a certain area of the lough shore there was an abundance of highly polished attractive stones.

They were known as 'Lough Neagh Pebbles' and were highly prized by the ancients for use as seals and in making necklaces.

Up until the early 1600s a large part of the area was covered by the fabulous forest of Glenconkeyne, dominated by oak trees. This immense forest stretched for about twenty miles along the western shore of Lough Neagh and about ten miles eastwards. Cookstown, which comprised only a few houses at that time, was surrounded by this wilderness. Local clansmen, especially the mighty O'Neills, Kings of Ulster, were able to use this vast forest as a place of refuge from the forces of the Crown. The various clans were not only continually at war with the militia but from time to time would be engaged in bitter conflict with each other in order to establish supremacy. An indication of the extent of the forest is the fact that in 1609 some 50000 oak, 100000 ash and 10000 elm were removed by permission of James I. This timber was shipped from Lough Neagh and taken, by way of the Lower Bann, for use in the building of Derry and Coleraine.

Oak wood was in great demand for the making of pipe staves for the growing Spanish wine trade and vast areas of the forest were cleared by settlers so that the land could be utilised for agriculture. Virtually all of this great forest has now disappeared, but the Drummond Oak still exists as a reminder of it. This mighty tree stands in a remote part of what was the Killymoon Estate at the south end of Cookstown. It is hundreds of years old and is a staggering 25 feet in circumference. It has iron stanchions as supports that must have been attached to it several centuries ago. The story has been passed down the generations that King William III, on his way to the Battle of the Boyne, encamped near it and tethered his horse to this giant of the arboreal world.

The peaty soil along the shores of the lough has preservative properties and massive pieces of bog oak have been unearthed, remnants of the forest of Glenconkeyne.

Since Lough Neagh is such a vast expanse of water, it is only natural that stories were told by the people of ancient times to explain its origins. One concerns the legendary Irish giant Finn McCool, leader of the renowned warriors, the Fianna. We are told that Finn was so enraged by a Scottish giant that he threw handfuls of earth at him and the resulting depression formed Lough Neagh. (The soil, which missed his adversary, landed in the Irish Sea and is now known as the Isle of Man.) Another ancient legend gives us a different explanation for the formation of the Lough. The story tells us that there was a well which was not to be left uncovered for fear of dire consequences. A woman went to fetch water and heard her child crying in its cradle. She rushed back to comfort the child but forgot to replace the cover on the well and the water flowed out so quickly it drowned the woman and child and formed the lough.

About eight miles from Cookstown is the village of Pomeroy. A mile from Pomeroy is King James' well where James II stopped to water his horse on his journey to the siege of Derry.

The earliest humans reached Ireland probably about 5000 BC, crossing the land bridge from Scotland, and there is ample proof of their existence from the discovery of the flint implements which they used. Evidence suggests that it was probably not until Neolithic times (3000 BC) that the area of mid-Ulster began to be colonised in significant numbers. By this time more sophisticated tools were made and used and considerable numbers of stone implements used by the early dwellers have been found in the sand-pits around Cookstown.

Certainly by the year 2000 BC, these early people were well established in Co. Tyrone. They had begun to spread from the forest-covered valleys, where they lived off fish from the rivers and game from the forest, to more elevated areas. Evidence of their existence is provided by their stone burial chambers, or megaliths, of which there were three main kinds: passage graves; horned cairns and gallery graves. Cist burial, which did not use a covering cairn, was also practised. At Loughry just on the southern outskirts of Cookstown the skeleton of a boy was uncovered about fifty years ago in an earth-lined cist, along with an ornate food vessel.

About six miles from Cookstown at the village of Coagh is an impressive dolmen. It comprises an enormous capstone weighing more than twenty tons supported on uprights of basalt about thirteen feet in height and is called the 'Tamlaght Stone'. As the word Tamlaght means 'plague grave', this would explain the significance of the structure. Near Pomeroy is the Cregganconroe Cairn which is an example of a horned cairn and close to Lough Fea is the Ballybriest Cairn, a double-horned cairn dating from Neolithic times. Not far from Davagh Forest, to the west of Cookstown, is the intriguing Beaghmore Stone Circle which was built on an older settlement also dating from the Neolithic period.

About thirty years ago, in the parish of Lissan just a few miles from Cookstown, a very important archeological discovery was made. Prior to this the earliest evidence of human habitation dated back to Neolithic times, but this find would appear to be an indication of the oldest Stone Age house in Ireland and Great Britain, dating back some 6000 years. There was also an accompanying find of artefacts which yielded useful information.

The ringed forts found in the area indicate the presence of early civilisations. The fort, just outside Cookstown at Tullyhogue, where the O'Neills of Ulster were crowned, was probably used thousands of years before by Neolithic people.

In prehistoric times animal species roamed Ireland which have long since disappeared from the island. Among them were red deer, reindeer, bears, lemmings, the Great Irish Deer and, in earlier times, even mammoths. The Great Irish Deer was certainly present in mid-Ulster, for evidence of it has been found in Lough Neagh and the Sperrin Mountains.

Cookstown, along with Strabane, was distinctive in Co. Tyrone for having two different railway companies operating to and from it. One was the L.M.S., which commenced operations in Cookstown in 1856, followed by the G.N.R. in 1879. The two companies had their own separate, adjacent stations contained within the same building and competition between them for custom was intense.

There were about seven passenger trains operating to and from Cookstown every day. Regular goods trains also proved a great boon for the commercial life of the town. To facilitate the loading of produce and livestock, the railway line extended from the station across Union Street into the Market Yard.

In 1885, the Prince and Princess of Wales, later King Edward VII and Queen Alexandra, had been to Northern Ireland on an official visit. Their train was obliged to stop at Cookstown to enable them to board a train going from the other station on their journey to Larne. It had been arranged for the Town Commissioners, forerunners of the Council, to greet the Royal personages when they disembarked to change trains. It fell to the Chairman of the Commissioners to make the speech welcoming Their Majesties to the town. To overcome his nervousness on this auspicious occasion, he had imbibed a few tots of spirits whilst waiting for the train from the bottle he had brought with him.

Consequently, when his important moment arrived, after a few false starts, he was unable to deliver the greeting. He resolved the difficulty by handing the speech, which was written on parchment, to the Prince saying, "Here you are Your Majesty, it will give you something to read on the train, and tell your mother I got many's a sore head drinking her health."

In 1929 the Easter Excursion return ticket from Cookstown to Belfast by train was: First Class, ten shillings (50p); Second class, 8 shillings (40p), Third Class, 6 shillings (30p).

The trains ceased operating in Cookstown in 1956. However the imposing railway station building has been retained: part of it was, until recently, used as the Tourist Office and the eye catching semi-circular iron structure with the G.N.R. logo still remains over the entrance to what is now the Town Council's Amenity Depot.

The Old Railway Station
COOKSTOWN

John. S. Higgan

The name Oldtown is self-explanatory. This is where the first houses of Cookstown were built by Dr. Allen Cooke, an English ecclesiastical lawyer, who obtained a lease of land in the area. Cooke was granted a charter by Charles I in 1628 to hold a Saturday market and two annual fairs, and the town came to be called Cookstown in his honour.

Looking north from the Oldtown Hill the Sperrin Mountains, some eight miles distant, dominate the landscape. From the Oldtown Hill, Milburn Street stretches to the Moneymore Road which runs east. This road is close to the town's northern limits.

Many of the houses in Milburn Street were factory houses. They were owned by the Gunnings who had a linen mill which utilised the water from a nearby burn. This explains how Milburn Street got its name. Halfway down Milburn Street, off the western side, is the Factory Lane which led to Milburn Linen Factory.

There is no factory at the bottom of the lane now, but generations of folk from Milburn Street have trodden up and down that lane to and from their work. In the morning the penetrating sound of the factory horn told the employees that it was time to be up and off to work or face a fine for being late. For those who did not work in the factory and did not relish the blaring of the horn it did at least enable them to check that their clocks were showing the correct time.

The high pitched blast of the steam-operated horn could be heard at seven o'clock in the morning and then again at eight o'clock. By that time the workers who came from Milburn Street and further afield were expected to be through the factory gates or pay the penalty for their tardiness.

Gradually, the linen industry went into decline and the factory gates closed for the last time in 1956. The loss of employment that the factory had provided for so many years caused temporary hardship until other work could be found and there was genuine sadness that an era had ended.

Oldtown

COOKSTOWN

John S. Haggan

Springhill is situated about a mile from Moneymore on the road to Coagh. It was built between 1680 and 1700 by the Conynghams who were a plantation family from Ayrshire in Scotland. They later changed their name to Lenox-Conyngham. The construction of the house was begun by William 'good Will' Conyngham and it is a fine example of the comfortable houses that replaced fortified castles in Ireland towards the end of the 17th century. As with many such properties, extensions were added to the house in the 18th and early 19th centuries.

'Good Will' Conyngham played a prominent part in the defence of Derry in 1689, leading a regiment which he had raised in his own locality. He later became a member of King William's Council of Six. Four flintlocks used in the Siege of Derry are preserved at Springhill and also on display is weaponry said to have been used in the 1798 rebellion at the battle of Vinegar Hill in Wexford.

A prominent feature of the Gun Room is its fine oak panelling. In the 1960s one of the panels had to be removed for repair and an exciting discovery was made. Beneath the panelling, the walls were covered with hand printed wallpaper, made in England about 1760, with a repeat design of a rustic folly framed by gothic arches. The design is printed in black and white on a grey-blue background.

The Blue Room is said to be haunted by the benign ghost of Olivia Lenox-Conyngham whose husband George died in the room in 1816.

There is also a fine library and a very interesting collection of 17th and 18th century objets d'art, including the medicine chest of the famous Duke of Marlborough, the hero of the Battle of Blenheim.

The house has charming gardens including the secluded herb garden which has an unusual Camomile lawn. To the rear of the house is a stand of impressive ancient yew trees which date back to the time of the great Glenconkeyne forest.

The property is now in the possession of the National Trust having been given to them by Captain William Lenox-Conyngham in 1959.

Springhill

MONEYMORE

John. S. Haggan

The Sperrin Mountains form an imposing backdrop to the village of Moneymore, about four miles to the north of Cookstown. The derivation of the name is uncertain: 'money' comes either from 'moin' meaning 'bog' or 'muine' meaning 'shrubbery', so Moneymore could mean large bog or large shrubbery. As the village was once surrounded by the vast forest of Glenconkeyne, the latter meaning might be more likely, but is open to conjecture. Whatever the name means, Moneymore is a pleasing plantation village with many charming architectural features. In order to preserve its unique character it is now a conservation area, which will ensure that changes cannot be made without careful consideration.

The village was founded and developed over a twenty year period in the early 1600s by the London Drapers' Company who put considerable thought into the planning of the village. Running water was supplied which was a remarkable innovation in those early times. The company provided the village with a market house, schools, an inn, a dispensary and dwellings that have stayed mainly unchanged though some have been put to other uses. The school house, for instance, is now the Orange Hall.

Close to Moneymore is Carndaisy wood and glen. The very name would entice you to visit it and it is an ideal place for a picnic. At Carndaisy is a well kept secret: a tortuous road winding almost to the summit of Slieve Gallion. For the intrepid adventurer, the reward is a breathtaking view of the surrounding countryside.

For the archaeologist, Ballymully long cairn is barely a mile to the west of Moneymore.

Moneymore Village

MONEYMORE POST OFFICE

John S Haggan

About ten miles north east of Cookstown, on the western shore of Lough Neagh, lies the pretty little village of Ballyronan, meaning O'Ronan's Town. To the south of the village stands Salter's Castle, a plantation castle built about 1619 by the Salter Company who were allocated a tract of land in the area. The castle has a dwelling house surrounded by a walled enclosure with circular towers.

Ballyronan can boast the earliest recorded spade mill in Northern Ireland which was in operation in 1780. Spades and coal boxes were made but the exact site of the mill is not clear. Other former industries include candle and soap making, tanning, brewing and distilling.

During the last century Ballyronan was an embarkation point for people emigrating from Derry and Tyrone to America to seek a new life. They set sail from here on the first stage of their journey.

Ballyronan had a busy flax mill which was operating until the 1950s. The flourishing linen industry was established at Ballyronan by the Hugenots, said to be the most skilful cloth makers in the world, who did much to revolutionise the linen industry in Ulster. The Hugenots came from north east France and Flanders but were obliged to leave their homeland due to the religious intolerance of Louis XIV. William III was quick to utilise the experience of these refugees to improve the efficiency of the linen industry. The main driving force behind the plan was Louis Crommelin, a tireless organiser. He was so success-ful that he is regarded as 'The Father of the Ulster Linen Industry'.

Ballyronan is now important for its marina. It caters for boating and a wide range of water sports including canoeing and water skiing. Boats can be hired and self catering accommodation is available.

Ballyronan

John S. Haggan

There are a number of attractive bridges over the River Ballinderry which flows past the south end of Cookstown. The Ballinderry Bridge is on the Coagh to Ballyronan Road and is the last bridge across the river before it reaches Lough Neagh. Near the bridge is a weir, used to provide water for a fish farm which produces rainbow trout.

All spawning fish have to pass under the Ballinderry Bridge. The members of the Ballinderry River Enhancement Association hope to put a fish counting mechanism just downstream from the bridge to enable them to gauge the success of their restocking programme. To provide additional information it is intended to put a video camera at the counting site. From the information the video provides, the Association will be able to gauge the size, sex and species of the fish.

The Association has been operating for eighteen years and the important conservation work that it does should not be underestimated. Through its constant monitoring of water quality it can help to ensure that rivers are kept in a healthy state and maintain a thriving fish population.

When the balance of nature is affected in a river this can have far-reaching, detrimental consequences for the fish population. If a problem arises the Association can investigate and take remedial action. Well-stocked rivers have important financial implications for they attract not only local anglers but also foreign tourists who come on fishing holidays.

The Association's work of breeding trout, dollaghan and salmon for release into the river is carried out at Orritor near Cookstown. This operation requires tremendous expertise but the success of this work can be gauged by the fact that in the Lissan Water alone the number of 'redds', or spawning places, has increased dramatically from 20 to 500. The Association also advises and gives practical help to other areas in the country.

An important part of the Association's work is educational and many groups of children visit their premises to learn about the various projects. This should help to promote an interest in conservation and ensure that the children become environmentally aware.

Ballinderry Bridge

John S Haggan

Coyle's Cottage is a fisherman's cottage on the western shore of Lough Neagh. It is about 300 years old and is in the townland of Aneeterbeg in Ardboe.

It was restored due to the efforts of Muinterevlin Historical Society who first held their meetings in a converted barn. The society decided to obtain the use of a derelict cottage for their meetings and work began with the aim of restoring it to its original state. It had one living room with part of the room curtained off for a kitchen area, four small windows and the customary half door. The whitewashed walls are made of mud and the corners are stone-built to strengthen the building.

The roof beams are made of bog oak which is around 2000 years old. This would have been found locally, buried in the peat which had preserved it. The presence of bog oak gives an indication of the vast oak forest which once covered a large part of Co. Tyrone.

As was the custom, the cottage is thatched with local Lough Neagh reed. It is the only reed thatched building in the area. The cottage is available to any community group as a meeting place.

The following poem is about a cottage in the vicinity of Cookstown. No-one can recall when it was lived in and originally it probably also had a thatched roof.

The Empty Cottage

The empty cottage stands there,
By a turning in the lane,
With moss encrusted slated roof,
In the windows not a pane.
The once gleaming white-washed walls,
Are flaked and stained with grime,
Ravaged now by long neglect,
And relentless passing time.
The garden, once a mother's joy,
With countless blooms arrayed,
Is now an unkempt wilderness,
Where rampart brambles spread.
How quickly have the years slipped by,
Since I with childhood pals,
That cottage our own secret haunt,
Romped within those walls.
Then once again that humble home,
With glee our voices filled,
Just as other children's had,
That now are long since stilled.

Eddie McCartney
(First published in the anthology 'Northern Ireland Poets'.)

Coyle's Cottage
ARDBOE

Almost ten miles to the east of Cookstown, on an elevated site near the shores of Lough Neagh, is Ardboe Old Cross. The name Ardboe comes from the Irish language and means 'hill of the cow'.

The cross dates from the 10th century and was probably the first High Cross to be erected in Ulster. It is eighteen and a half feet high and the arms are three and a half feet wide. Vital repairs to the structure were carried out in 1817 and 1846 by Colonel Stewart who lived in Killymoon Castle.

The cross has 22 panels which are decorated with carvings of biblical scenes. Unfortunately, due to the ravages of the weather, some of the pictures are badly worn and difficult to interpret. On the western side there are scenes from the Old Testament such as the stories of Adam and Eve and the Sacrifices of Isaac. The east side deals with the New Testament and one panel shows the Visit of the Magi. Amongst the scenes depicted on the south side is David struggling with the lion. The scenes on the north side are more difficult to interpret.

Nearby is the Abbey which was founded by St. Colman in 590. In the 18th century pilgrims visited the cross to pray. There was also a belief that the waters of the lough had healing powers.

According to local legend, when the cross was being built, a magic cow emerged from the lough and sustained the workers with supplies of cream, milk and butter until the erection of the cross was completed.

The Old Cross
ARDBOE

John S Haggas

The picturesque village of Coagh is situated five miles east of Cookstown on the Ballinderry River. The village, which was founded in the 1720s, grew up at a fording point on the Ballinderry. It is about five miles from the harbour of Newport Trench, known locally as the Battery, on the western shore of Lough Neagh. The name Coagh comes from the Irish word 'an uiach' meaning 'the hollow'.

The main feature of the village is the impressive Hanover Square. It was named in honour of the reigning Hanoverian King George II by George Conyngham of Springhill after the king had granted a charter to hold a weekly market and four annual fairs. Conyngham was responsible for building the fine six-arch bridge over the River Ballinderry which still stands today.

Coagh has, it seems, always been a thriving village. An Ordnance Survey report dated 1840 illustrates that Coagh was a self-sufficient, prosperous place, despite the fact that its market folded due to the proximity of the larger market at Cookstown where higher prices for stock and produce could be obtained.

We are told that: "The loss of a weekly market is not materially felt by the inhabitants as the shopkeepers and tradespeople are a very respectable class. They do not derive their entire support from their establishments having in general farms in the immediate vicinity of the town and also the poorer classes can purchase from the farmer on the most reasonable terms. Their shops are always well supplied with goods of the best quality. Wheatmeal, oatmeal and bran is in constant supply in the grocers' shops."

A comprehensive range of agricultural implements was available. A foundry spade could be bought for 2 shillings (10p). The 1840 report continues that a corn mill had been there from time immemorial; the present owner being one, Duncan Storey. There was also a flax mill at Urbal owned by Thomas Duff.

Coagh has progressed but still retains its old world charm. In the square is one of Coagh's finest buildings, Hanover House. Now a hotel, it still retains its original attractive facade. Anglers know that the fishing in the Ballinderry River at Coagh is exceptional. Nearby is the large dolmen called the Tamlaght Stone.

Coagh Bridge

John S. Haggan

If you had been strolling along the river bank near Coagh Weir more than eighty years ago, you may well have encountered a young boy called Hammy Kennedy who was a keen angler. Hammy might have been fond of fishing but, like his brother Jimmy, his real passion was music and both went on to gain international recognition as songwriters.

Among the songs that Hammy wrote or co-wrote were 'Ole Faithful', 'How can you buy Killarney?' and 'The Shawl of Galway Grey': popular songs on both sides of the Atlantic and recorded by such famous singers as Gene Autry and Joseph Lock. Hammy was a part-time writer but it became Jimmy's vocation and he went on to become one of the world's leading songwriters especially during the 1930s & 1940s.

It was in Coagh that Jimmy displayed early promise as a composer. As a youth he played the organ in Tamlaght Parish Church and after services he would play voluntaries that he had spontaneously composed. Jimmy attended Coagh village school and later Cookstown Academy, a small grammar school which closed many years ago.

Jimmy gained a B.A. from Trinity College, Dublin but, despite being well qualified to embark on a secure career, songwriting was his ambition. He eventually gained international success with 'South of the Border' which was first recorded by Gene Autry. The range of songs that Jimmy Kennedy wrote is truly remarkable. They include 'Harbour Lights', 'My Prayer', 'The Isle of Capri' and 'Does your Mother come from Ireland?' which was a particular favourite of Bing Crosby. Others who have recorded Jimmy's songs include Gracie Fields, Frank Sinatra and Nat King Cole. Jimmy died in 1984 aged 82.

He has been admitted to ' The Music Hall of Fame', the highest accolade that can be accorded any song writer. No other Irish-born songwriter has ever been granted this honour.

Coagh Weir

Ballyclog Church is on the Coagh to Stewartstown road and it is well worth stopping to admire this fine old building with its attractive architectural features. On the other side of the road are the remains of the original church which was abandoned in 1868.

Around the original church is the old graveyard. At one time there was a shrine, embellished with gold and silver, which contained the bronze Bell of St. Patrick. During penal times, the shrine and bell were kept in safe hiding places by local clan leaders. The shrine is now housed in the National Museum in Dublin.

A former rector of the church was the Rev. Charles Wolfe who also ministered at another Co. Tyrone church, Donaghmore. Wolfe is famous for writing the poem, 'The Burial of Sir John Moore' which has been included in innumerable anthologies over the years and was familiar to generations of children. Sir John Moore was an English general who was killed in the battle against the French at Corunna in the Peninsular War.

Wolfe was inspired to write the poem after reading an account of the battle by Robert Southey for 'The Annual Register' and it was first published in the 'Newry Telegraph'.

Charles Wolfe attended Trinity College, Dublin, as did his more famous cousin, the charismatic Wolfe Tone, who was a Presbyterian and the leader of the United Irishmen in the 1798 rebellion.

Charles Wolfe studied theology and Wolfe Tone's studies led him into the legal profession. Charles Wolfe was plagued by indifferent health. Following his death from consumption at the early age of 32, he was buried at Youghal. Wolfe Tone's grave is at Bodenstown.

The first and last verses of 'The Burial of Sir John Moore' are:

'Not a drum was heard, not a funeral note
As his corpse to the rampart we hurried,
Not a soldier discharges his farewell shot,
O'er the grave where our Hero we buried.

We buried him darkly at dead of night,
The sods with our bayonets turning,
By the struggling moonbeam's misty light,
And the lantern dimly burning.'

Ballyclog Church

John S Haggan

Stewartstown, about five miles south east of Cookstown, is a former market town built around a large square. It was founded early in the 17th century by Sir Arthur Stuart, who had been granted a vast parcel of land in the area by James I. Stuart Hall was built close to the town about 1760 by John Stewart and was the seat of the Earl of Castlestewart. (The family name seems to have been spelt both as Stewart and Stuart over the years.)

Close to Stewartstown is Creeve Lough with its crannog. Crannog comes from the word 'crann', meaning 'tree', and refers to a wooden construction. In earlier times a basket used for carrying corn was called a crannog. In the topographical sense, the word is used to refer to wooden houses placed on an artificial island in a lake. These islands were constructed in shallow water by hammering poles into the lake bottom. Cross beams were affixed to the poles. On these would be piled a conglomeration of material such as clay, brambles and small trees until an island was formed where a family, sometimes several families, lived in wooden houses. This mode of habitation provided some protection from enemies. The occupants stayed on the crannog at night and reached the shore in small boats. The word crannog has now generally come to mean the whole construction, both the island and the houses. Lake dwellings such as these were lived in from the remotest times until the 17th century.

Some local place names are derived from the word crannog, although the lake and the artificial island have long since disappeared. for instance, the townland of Crannoge, near the village of Pomeroy.

About a mile to the west of Stewartstown is Roughan Lough which can also boast a crannog. Near the lough is Roughan Castle which was erected about 1618 by Arthur Stewart.

The crannog on Roughan Lough is of particular historical significance. The power of the O'Neills, Kings of Ulster for centuries, finally came to an end on this crannog when Sir Phelim O'Neill, a leading participant in the 1641 rebellion, was captured there and taken to Dublin to be hanged.

Creeve Lough
STEWARTSTOWN

A few miles south of Cookstown is Lindsayville Row, a charming group of listed houses named after the Lindsay family who resided at the manor in nearby Loughry Estate.

A frequent guest of the Lindsay family was Jonathan Swift, one of the most distinguished men of letters of his time. Swift was fearlessly critical of those who incurred his displeasure and no-one, whatever their rank, escaped the lash of his tongue or the vitriol of his pen if he felt it was deserved. Naturally this did not endear the irascible Swift to the Establishment and explains why he did not rise higher than Dean of St. Patrick's in the church hierarchy, to which position he was appointed in 1713. Dean Swift was greatly admired by the ordinary people of Dublin who were very upset when he died, aged 87, in 1754.

At Loughry he would spend much of his time writing in the garden arbour and the arbour is now known as Dean Swift's Cottage. His best known book, 'Gulliver's Travels' is regarded as a children's classic although it was intended as a political satire.

You may have heard the song about Phelim Brady called 'The Bard of Armagh'. One version begins,

"Oh! list to the strains of a poor Irish harper.
And scorn not the strings from his poor withered hand.
Remember his fingers could once move more sharper.
And raise up the praise of his dear native land".

Phelim Brady's real name was Dr. Patrick Donnelly. He had been ordained by Archbishop Plunkett of Armagh at Dundalk in 1673 and was appointed Bishop of Dromore. Owing to the repressive laws against non-conformists, he travelled about disguised as Phelim Brady, a harper. His true identity was suspected and he was imprisoned in Dublin. When released he continued with his duties until his death in 1716. We are told that his body was moved under cover of darkness to be buried in the family plot at Desertcreat Parish Church, near Loughry. A stone slab marks the grave but the inscription is now almost indecipherable. As the graveyard dates back to before the reformation, people of different persuasions were interred there.

Built into the porch of Desertcreat Church is said to be a piece of the throne on which the O'Neills of Ulster were crowned at Tullyhogue Fort.

Lindsayville Row
DESERTCREAT

About two miles to the south of Cookstown, near Tullyhogue village, is Tullyhogue Fort or rath, Tullyhogue meaning 'the hill of the youth'. Due to its connections with the O'Neills, the Kings of Ulster, this is one of the most important historic sites in Ireland. The O'Neills, who were a dominant family in Ireland for about five hundred years, were traditionally crowned at Tullyhogue Fort, it being the clan seat of the O'Hagans who were hereditary stewards to the O'Neills. An early map indicates a crude throne made of stone slabs and also shows thatched houses which have long since disappeared. The circular fort, which is 100 feet across, was apparently entered by a passage from the north. It is situated at an elevation of some 600 feet with a commanding view of the surrounding countryside.

During the inauguration the O'Neill was crowned in an elaborate ceremony, conducted by the Primate of Armagh, who instructed the participants on their duties. There was a procession to the hill and its arrival was proclaimed by a band of trumpeters. When the procession reached the throne, the O'Neill seated himself on it and the rules by which he was to govern were read out to him by the chief bard, whereupon he affirmed his acceptance of this code by swearing his compliance on the Bell of St. Patrick. To demonstrate that he would not govern his people corruptly or with force he set aside his sword and battle dress and accepted a rod or white wand.

When all the remaining rituals were completed the new King was cheered by the thousands of spectators. The festivities then began in which the playing of harps figured prominently.

The last O'Neill to be crowned on the throne of stone was the great Hugh O'Neill in 1595. After his downfall the throne was smashed on the orders of the Lord Lieutenant Mountjoy in a policy of destroying clan symbols.

Ringed forts are a common feature in this part of the country. They were usually about 50 to 100 feet across and some had the surrounding earth mound reinforced with stones. Townland names often help to identify forts: the terms 'dun', 'rath' and 'liss' indicate earth-banked forts whilst 'cathair' or 'caiseal' refer to stone-walled forts.

Tullyhogue Fort

John. S. Haggan

A few miles to the east of Cookstown off the Cloghog Road, Drapersfield is a quiet backwater on the River Ballinderry. The small community grew up round the linen factory and, when linen manufacture ceased, the factory, for a time, produced berets. The residence of the factory owners, Drapersfield House, is now a private nursing home in an idyllic, tranquil rural setting.

The weir at Drapersfield was constructed to provide water power for driving the machinery when the linen mill was in operation. There are many weirs along the River Ballinderry built to provide water power for a variety of purposes: for scutching flax, producing linen, milling corn and generating electricity.

One such weir was built by an enterprising farmer upstream from Drapersfield and not far from Drum Manor, where the Close family lived. The farmer had a scutch mill and the electricity that he generated provided light for his dwelling and farm buildings. He made an agreement with the Close family to supply electricity and he duly erected poles for the line to carry the power to Drum Manor House. The upper classes visited each other on a regular basis for wining and dining and the Close family frequently entertained others of the landed gentry.

On one occasion there was a convivial evening held at Drum Manor House. The festivities extended into the wee small hours then suddenly, at the height of the merriment, the lights went out. The farmer who had supplied the electricity to the Manor House was wakened at an unearthly hour by frantic knocking on his door. A servant had been despatched to see if he could (literally!) throw any light on the situation. The gentleman, who was of a sanguine nature and not easily discommoded, soon rectified the problem. Illumination was restored to Drum Manor House and the carousing continued unabated until the crack of dawn.

Drapersfield Weir

John S. Haggan

Killymoon Castle is almost a mile to the east of Cookstown, near the northern bank of the River Ballinderry. The original castle was built in 1671 by James Stewart on the substantial demesne which had been granted to him under the Plantation settlement, but it was destroyed by fire in 1801. In 1802 Colonel William Stewart had a new, more imposing castle built, designed by John Nash, the famous London architect.

The Colonel was determined that his residence should rival the finest in Ireland and no expense was spared. It was built to resemble a Norman castle and cost the colossal sum of £80000, which was an amazing amount of money in those days. The Stewarts were renowned for their hospitality and the castle was famous for the lavish feasts and functions held in its magnificent ballroom. The elite of the nobility regarded it a privilege to be entertained at Killymoon Castle.

Even royalty came to stay. On one occasion the Prince Regent was visiting the castle when it was owned by James, son of Colonel William Stewart. James was an inveterate gambler and he and the Prince sat up all night playing cards. Stewart was losing heavily and the stakes grew higher and higher. The story goes that eventually the hapless Stewart lost everything, including the castle, to his guest. However the next day the Prince told Stewart that he would not insist on his honouring the debt and made disparaging remarks about the fine property that he had won.

In 1917, Killymoon estate was owned by a remarkable gentleman, a native of Cork, Dr. Gerald Macaura, though it is doubtful that his title of doctor was authentic. He had made a fortune from a machine he had invented which was supposed to have miraculous powers of healing. The resourceful Macaura brought lumberjacks from Canada to fell the trees on the estate, convinced that another fortune was to be made from the timber, but soon discovered that he had miscalculated. Mysteriously, the enormous stack of timber went up in flames but the insurers would not pay compensation.

The castle and the estate were sold and the castle which had cost £80000 to build was purchased by a local man for £100.

Killymoon Castle

Tullagh Bridge, on the Ballinderry River, is just to the west of Cookstown. It is very old and its use as a crossing point has been superceded by more recent bridges. As it is not easily accessible, there may be some townspeople who do not know its exact location and many would certainly doubt its safety.

Cookstown today has excellent indoor swimming facilities. Years ago, before these were available, local boys learned to swim at various places on the Ballinderry River. Near the bridge were some very popular locations. On hot summer days boys would make the long trek out of town up Tullagh Road (Tullagh meaning 'hill'), down the steep Tullagh Lane and along the river bank to the place where they would practise their aquatic skills.

Along the river a wide range of birds could be seen that are sadly not so common nowadays. Sand martins nested in holes in one particular bank. There were also moorhens; grey wagtails, yellow in colour; kingfishers and dippers with their characteristic white breast and apparently uncontrollable nod.

Minnows could be caught using a pound jam-pot with a string tied round its neck. Boys who were versed in the intricacies of minnow catching knew to fill the jar with water before tossing it into the river so that it would sink to the bottom, otherwise, frustratingly, it might just bob about. When the jam-pot was hauled in, there was usually a minnow in it which did not have the wit to escape from the pot the way it had got in.

By the Ballinderry River
I would often stroll,
And the peacefulness around me,
How it soothed my soul.
There I saw the kingfisher
With jewelled plumage bright,
Perched motionless above a pool
Flecked with dappled light.
The cattle drowsed above the bank
Where the ash and alder grow,
And speckled trout swam lazily
'Gainst the river's gentle flow.
The moorhen fussed around her brood
That paddled here and there.
She, calling to them anxiously,
They, without a care.
And though life's stream has carried me
Far from that pleasant place,
Fondly, in my memory,
There I my steps retrace.

Eddie McCartney
(First published in the anthology 'Northern Ireland Poets'.)

Tullagh Bridge

Cottages as we know them date only from about.1600. They gradually evolved from a single room to sometimes three rooms, including two bedrooms and a kitchen. To save space, smaller cottages had a curtained-off outshot (alcove) beside the hearth containing a double bed. Some cottages had a loft, reached by a ladder, to provide additional sleeping space. Where there was a loft there was a small gable window to provide some light.

The open turf fire had a crane on which the kettle and cooking pots were hung. The furniture was sparse, the most important item being the dresser. The kitchen floor was flagged or, in more primitive cottages, simply beaten earth.

Cottages were thatched with whatever materials were available. Flax or wheatstraw were popular in many areas but along the Lough Neagh shore, the cottagers used the reeds that grow in abundance. A fine example of reed thatching is the lovingly restored Coyle's Cottage. The thatch was held in place by scallops which could be made from willow, laurel, hazel, briar or, in later years, wire. On many cottages the thatch was later replaced by slates, as has happened on this cottage in the townland of Orritor.

A well constructed cottage would have had random stonework covered with lime plaster. The plaster was made from burnt lime slaked with water and allowed to mature, then mixed with sand. To strengthen the mixture, animal hair and ox blood could be added. When several layers of this mixture were smoothed over the walls it made a remarkably resilient coating that was impervious to all weathers. Windows were usually sited on the front wall and some cottages had a half door which could be opened to provide additional light.

Dotted through the countryside are the remnants of small cottages whose inhabitants eked out a precarious existence before crossing the Atlantic in search of the American dream.

Cottage at Orritor

John S. Haggan

About four miles west of Cookstown on the River Kildress, situated in a quiet glen in the townland of Corkhill, is Wellbrook Beetling Mill. Beetling is the stage of linen manufacture in which the cloth is beaten with heavy wooden hammers by an intricate mechanism to give it its characteristic shine before being bleached.

The beetling mill was part of a complex that included the bleaching of linen, but later operated as an independent business. For this reason, Wellbrook Beetling Mill was still in operation almost a century after bleaching had ceased at the complex.

The bleaching operation at Wellbrook was started about 1764 by a linen merchant called Hugh Faulkner who lived in Cookstown at Gortlowry. At that time linen production was a cottage industry and the weavers spun and wove the cloth and then brought it to the markets where it would be purchased by merchants like Hugh Faulkner for beetling and selling on for bleaching. Faulkner could see that greater profit could be made if he had a bleaching process of his own where he could finish the cloth ready to sell at the cloth halls in Dublin or to English merchants.

When Faulkner was searching for a suitable site he took his fishing rod with him so that no-one would suspect his real reason for scouting along the river bank and perhaps take advantage of his idea.

In the final stages of setting up his operation, Faulkner, in order to get the job completed, plied the workmen liberally with whiskey. He tells us that they "drank whiskey from eight to nine and fought from nine to eleven". There were no serious injuries, just a few shirts and waistcoats torn. He observed that mountainy men were inclined to fight when they got drunk, an understatement if ever there was one. However, the work was completed satisfactorily, which is remarkable considering 15 gallons of whiskey were consumed in the process!

The Wellbrook Beetling Mill was acquired by the National Trust in 1969 and it is important as the only Beetling Mill that can be seen operating in Northern Ireland. Within the property there is also an interesting display of other aspects of the linen industry.

Wellbrook Beetling Mill
CORKHILL

About three miles west of Cookstown, on the road to Omagh, is Drum Manor Forest Park. It is well maintained with many captivating features all within easy reach of each other. In 1964 the property was acquired by the Forestry Division of the Ministry of Agriculture and it was eventually opened to the public in 1970. The park grounds have been carefully developed to make it a fascinating place to visit with amenities to suit everyone.

Drum Manor has connections with one of the most famous of Ulster families. It is situated in an area which was once part of the territory of the O'Hagans who acted as stewards for the O'Neills, the Kings of Ulster.

After the 1641 rebellion, the land was forfeited to the Crown. Kildress Parish, which included Drum Manor, was later granted by Charles I to Mr R. Richardson and for some time was actually known as Manor Richardson.

By the early 18th century the family's name had become Richardson-Brady, presumably due to the marriage of a lady of the Richardson line to a Brady.

In 1860 Augusta La Vicompte Richardson-Brady married Hugh Massey, a major in the 85th Foot Regiment.

After Major Massey's death, his widow married Henry James Viscount Stewart, who was later 5th Earl of Castlestewart, in 1866. The marriage took place by special licence at Oaklands House, which was the name of Drum Manor at the time.

One of their two daughters, Lady Muriel Albany Stewart, married Maxwell Archibald Close, a major in the 13th Regiment of Hussars, in 1891. The Manor was acquired by the Forestry Division from the late Maxwell Archibald Close M.A., the second son of the original Maxwell Archibald Close.

Beech Walk
DRUM MANOR

The eastern part of the Manor House was begun in 1829. It was later extended and the completed manor dates from 1876. The roof has unfortunately had to be removed and within the walls a most attractive garden has been laid out. In the tea-room, pictures of the manor in its original state are on display.

The ornamental ponds are stocked with trout and here you will see wildfowl including mallard duck and mute swans.

A special feature is the Butterfly Garden which was laid out by Dr. Henry Heal, a noted lepidopterist. The garden has an extensive variety of wild flowers and shrubs which attract butterflies. This area is an important addition to the park as over the years there has been a serious decline in the number of butterflies that were once common. However here you have an opportunity of spotting such species as the Small Tortoiseshell, the Red Admiral, the Peacock, the Green-Veined White and others.

Near the Manor look out for the mammoth Western Hemlock tree. This specimen has the largest girth of any of its type in Ireland.

There are four different trails of varying distances to be taken. One of the walks accommodates the less able and is suitable for wheel-chair users.

On the Forest Plot Trail the Forest Service has planted a considerable variety of native and exotic trees as an educational feature. Red squirrels and their American cousins, grey squirrels, have both been sighted at Drum.

The Forest Park is open every day of the year from 8am until dusk. It provides a comprehensive range of services including a caravan site, camp site, picnic and barbecue area, tea-room, bookable guided tours for organised groups and facilities for the disabled as well as special events and facilities for wedding photographs.

The Pond
DRUM MANOR

Rock, just a few miles from Cookstown, is one of the many small villages to be found throughout the district. Set amongst the fields and byways of Co. Tyrone, these villages are quiet retreats. They are tidy and neat and are the very essence of peace and tranquillity. If you arrive at one of them you will surely be tempted to stop and linger for a while for, although they are small, they are all different and exude an appealing, timeless atmosphere.

'The Rock' has all these qualities and it has its pump which adds to the village's air of old world charm. The pump reminds us that not so long ago many places did not have the amenity of water on tap.

Certainly in Cookstown, as recently as the immediate post-war period, many of the houses in the main street relied on pumps, placed at intervals along the pavements, for their water supply.

These pumps, besides having a utilitarian function, were extremely attractive to look at. They had fluted columns surmounted by a heavy rounded top. When the handle was turned, water gushed out of the spout, which was shaped like a lion's head, streaming out of its permanently gaping jaws.

The top could be removed so that the mechanism would be accessible for repair. As each pump supplied water for a number of houses, it was a serious inconvenience if it failed to function properly, but this was a rare occurrence.as they were made to cope with unlimited turnings of the handle.

In the winter, to prevent it from freezing, each pump was wrapped with plaited straw, held in place by tightly-bound sacking. And there it stood, impervious to the frost, with only the lion's head and the handle, polished by the countless hands that had turned it over the years, protruding from the snugly fitting protective jacket.

The pump at the Rock, like all communal pumps, was a great meeting place where the women could exchange tit-bits of gossip as they took it in turn to fill their enamel buckets.

Village Green
ROCK

John S Haggan

In the heart of Co. Tyrone are countless scenes to captivate the eye in quiet places that are largely unknown. One such is this spell-binding dell of bluebells at Slate Quarry, near the road leading from Cookstown to Pomeroy.

The village of Pomeroy is set in the Altmore Hills which form part of the Sperrin Mountains, Altmore meaning 'great glen side'.

Pomeroy, at an altitude of more than 500 feet above sea level, has the distinction of being the highest village in Northern Ireland. It is among the most notable of the villages dotted through the Sperrins.

A gentleman by the name of Trimble was instrumental in the foundation of Pomeroy in the late 18th century. This information is denoted on his gravestone which is to be found in the Presbyterian burial ground.

The village takes its name from a family called Pomeroy who were granted a considerable number of townlands in the area during the time of the Plantation. The estate was later purchased by John Lowry and he built the large mansion which is known locally as Lowry's Castle. It was later acquired by the Department of Agriculture for use as a Forestry School.

In former times an important event in the village was the twice-yearly Hiring Fair, held in May and November. Men and women from the surrounding countryside would gather at the fair and hire themselves out to work as farm labourers and servants.

In the attractive little square is the Anglican Church which dates from the early 1840s. The belfry and the tower of the church were provided by the members of the Lowry family as a token of their esteem for Pomeroy, their birth-place.

On the outskirts of the village are the remains of a castle built in Elizabethan times by Sir Thomas Norris. Nearby is the well where James II stopped to drink on his way to the Siege of Derry in 1689.

There are a number of interesting archaeological sites in the vicinity, including Cregganconroe Cairn.

The grandfather of James Irwin, the Apollo 15 astronaut who landed on the moon in 1971, was born near Pomeroy and there are still family connections in the area.

Slate Quarry
(Bluebell Wood)
Pomeroy

This scene is near An Creagán Visitors' Centre which is situated off the main Cookstown to Omagh Road.

Cutting the turf for fuel was a necessary annual occupation. Each farm had its own turf bank in the nearest bog. Traditionally, cutting the turf would begin about the end of May, at a time of the year when there was normally a temporary lull in other farming activities.

When starting a new turf bank, the surface area would have to be cleared away to reach the peat underneath. A special spade would be used for cutting the sods with a narrower blade than normal and a flange at one side which made the job easier. The turves were laid out on the top of the bank. When one level had been cut another was started and a turf bank could have a number of levels.

The upper level of turf was brownish in colour and with each succeeding level the turf became blacker and blacker as the material was increasingly more compact. The turves were stacked in a special manner so that they would not easily topple over and the wind could dry them. Sometimes the turves were made into 'footings' to dry, which involved leaning them against one another at an angle. When dry, the turf was built into 'clamps', or 'stacks' which were larger. The final task would be to load the turf onto horse or donkey-drawn carts to be transported home.

Adjacent to An Creagán Visitors' Centre is 'The Black Bog', which is the largest raised bog in Northern Ireland. It is up to twelve metres deep. There are two types of bog: raised bogs and blanket bogs. Raised bogs were formed in shallow lakes about 12000 years ago. As plants died and sank to the bottom, successive layers of material were built up and gradually compressed to form the peat. Blanket bogs developed much later and were formed on land. They are usually shallower - up to three metres in depth.

Bogs are an important part of our natural heritage and it is important that they should be conserved. An Creagán Visitors' Centre has developed an excellent educational programme which enables people, especially children, to increase their knowledge of all aspects of bogs.

Turf Cutting
Creggan

About ten miles to the west of Cookstown, beside Davagh Forest Park, are the renowned Beaghmore Stone Circles. This extensive site, covering nearly one and a half acres, is one of the most famous archaeological discoveries in the whole of Ireland. The visitor can only stand and gaze in wonder at the site which dates from the early Bronze Age.

Beaghmore means a large grove of birch trees. 'Beagh' is derived from the Gaelic word 'beith' meaning 'birch tree'. A considerable number of place names show similar derivations such as Bahagh, Behagh and Behy.

The enigmatic site has seven circles; three pairs of circles and one other. There are about a dozen stone alignments running in a north east direction, perhaps towards the mid-summer sunrise, and a number of cairns. There are much smaller sites in the vicinity of Beaghmore which are comparable but not as spectacular.

As is usual in Ulster stone circles, the stones, in the main, are not very high. However, at Beaghmore there is one ring which has quite tall orthostats and within it several hundred small pointed stones.

The cairns cover burial cists. In some of the cists cremated bone was found and on the site a porcellanite axe head has been uncovered.

This remarkable site, which dates from about 4000 years ago, remained hidden under a layer of peat until it was first discovered a mere fifty years ago.

Local amateur archaeologist, the late George Barnett, was largely instrumental in discovering and excavating Beaghmore Circles. He spent considerable time and energy trying to interpret the meaning of the arrangement of stones. The experts are still uncertain as to why the ancients constructed this complex arrangement of stones at Beaghmore all those thousands of years ago. One theory is that the stones were placed to make astronomical measurements but the most popular current theory is that that the site pertains to fertility rites.

Preliminary investigations reveal that there are further archaeological mysteries, concealed under the peat of the moor, waiting to be uncovered.

Beaghmore Stone Circles

Glenlark is one of those remote, isolated places in the Sperrin Mountains, hardly known even to people who visit the Sperrins regularly.

The Sperrins have so many attractions that it is possible to go there time and time again and come away refreshed and fulfilled without having left the beaten track. But there have always been people with an urge to strike out across the mountains on foot to reach hidden places and experience the pleasure of trekking across the varied landscape. There are miles of unspoilt countryside, with meandering streams, gentle ridges, rounded hills, winding valleys and fast-flowing rivers, for the Sperrins are the largest and possibly the least-explored range of mountains in Ulster.

Walking in the Sperrins need not be confined to the experienced trekker. Various organisations have joined forces to ensure that everyone can enjoy the pleasure of exploring the area on foot. A new Sperrin Walking Festival Brochure has been produced, full of routes that will suit the casual and the experienced walker alike. Rambling in the Sperrins has attracted people in ever-increasing numbers and, in 1997, nearly 1000 people took part in the various organised walks.

There are a number of walking events which include Golden Sperrins Walking Weekend, Cookstown District Walking Festival and The Sperrins Hillwalking Festival. The festivals have walks to suit everyone so that families, beginners and experienced ramblers can all participate. The walks are conducted by knowledgeable guides

A trek down the Glenlark valley to Leckin is included among the large number of possible routes.

Glenlark Valley

Owenkillew River not only provides excellent fishing, like all rivers in the Sperrin Mountains, but it also contains traces of gold.

There is ample evidence to suggest that, in Ireland, gold was used for making ornaments as long ago as the Bronze Age, about 2000 years ago. Gold was obtained from alluvial soils or panned from the gravel of streams and rivers and was found in various places such as the district of Avoca in Wicklow as well as in the Sperrins.

Objects made from Irish gold have been found as far away as Egypt which indicates the existence of established trade routes. The catalogue of the National Museum in Dublin lists sufficient objects to show that gold was used in abundance for making ornaments, though this is only a fraction of what originally existed as tombs were often looted.

One of the treasures in the National Museum is St. Patrick's Bell shrine. It dates from the early 11th century and is decorated with gold. This shrine housed the bell that rang out when the O'Neills were crowned at Tullyhogue and it is generally assumed that the gold used to decorate the bell came from the Sperrins. During penal times the bell and shrine were kept in hiding in Co. Tyrone before the shrine eventually came into the possession of the museum.

Dr. Gerald Boate remarked in his book 'Ireland's Natural History', published in 1652, that he had gathered a gram of gold in the Sperrins and concluded that there could be a rich source of the precious metal.

A modern expert, Heuser, stated from his findings that enough gold could be extracted from the Mourne river valley system to make the project economically viable. The main concern for many people would be that such a project might be detrimental to the environment.

One of a number of Bronze Age gold lunulae, or neck ornaments, that have been found was discovered in the Cookstown District at Cregganconroe near Pomeroy. In 1816 a Bronze Age cloak and sleeve fasteners made of Sperrin gold were found hidden in a bank on the Killymoon estate. This significant and exciting find is known as the 'Killymoon Hoard'.

The Sperrin Heritage Centre, Plumbridge, has natural history and gold mining exhibits. If you want to have a go at panning for gold yourself, the centre can supply the equipment and advice!

Owenkillew River
GORTIN

The Glenelly River, in the heart of the Sperrin Mountains, flows through the scenic Glenelly Valley, past the little hamlets of Sperrin and Cranagh and the village of Plumbridge. The Glenelly River is only one of the fast-flowing, rocky-bedded rivers that add to the outstanding beauty of the Sperrins.

Goles Bridge crosses the river close to the very attractive Goles Forest., a popular spot for walkers.

The area is renowned not only for its scenery, but also because its rivers and loughs provide some of the best fishing in Europe for both game and coarse fish. The Glenelly River is particularly noted for its brown trout, salmon and sea trout.

Cookstown is on the Ballinderry River which drains into Lough Neagh. The Ballinderry provides excellent fishing and has more than 30 miles of bank to choose from. It is plentifully stocked and managed by the Ballinderry River Enhancement Association. The river is especially noted for its brown trout, dollaghan and salmon. Dollaghan is a unique species of Lough Neagh migratory brown trout which can be caught when they run the main tributaries from the middle of July until the end of October. Dollaghan are similar to salmon and grow up to three pounds every year while in the lough.

The waters of the Sperrin water system provide excel-
lent year-round coarse fishing with roach, bream, perch, pike, eels and hybrids to be caught.

Lough Neagh itself has an excellent stock of perch, pollan, bream, rudd, pike and, of course eels.

Near the Lough shore is Kinturk Cultural Centre where the visitor can learn all about Lough Neagh and its surroundings.

Goles Bridge
GLENELLY RIVER

John S Haggan

About ten miles to the north of Cookstown, along the B162, is the plantation town of Draperstown. Close to the River Moyola, the town looks towards Mullaghmore Mountain to the north and, to the south, Slieve Gallion.

About halfway between Cookstown and Draperstown lies the secluded Lough Fea. This enchanting little lough is an ideal place to pause for a ramble round the shores or for a picnic.

Draperstown was formerly known as the Cross of Ballinascreen ('Townland of the Shrubbery'). It developed as a market and post town and in 1818 its name was changed from Cross to Draperstown. By that time it was mostly in the possession of the London Drapers' Company. It was incumbent on the company to make improvements to the town and they were responsible for constructing a large market house and hotel. They also provided a dispensary for their tenants, built of freestone in the Elizabethan style.

Rights for a market were granted in 1792 and Draperstown is still famous for its flourishing market which attracts people from near and far.

The ruins of an ancient church are situated in the locality, in a secluded mountain glen at Moneyconey ('The Shrubbery of the Firewood'). The glen is reputed to have links with St. Patrick and the founding of the church is attributed to Columcille.

At Draperstown is the Plantation of Ulster Visitors Centre, one of the most innovative projects in the country. The Plantation of Ulster was a notable event in Irish history and the centre uses state-of-the-art technology to explore and explain the impact of the plantation and the events and personalities connected with it.

A mile from the town is the Rural College. Situated in 250 acres of woodland, it has been established as an educational and development resource, catering for groups and individuals from the United Kingdom, Republic of Ireland and Europe who wish to learn more about local development.

Market Day
DRAPERSTOWN

John S. Haggard

Rising in the background of the picture is Mount Sawel. There is some debate on how the peak came to be known as Sawel. One theory is that the name commemorates St. Patrick and is derived from Saul, the area close to Downpatrick where the saint established his first church in a barn. The barn was given to Patrick by the local chief Dichu whom Patrick had converted to Christianity. The word Saul comes from the Gaelic meaning 'barn'.

Although the numerous peaks of the Sperrin Mountains stretch along the entire west of Co. Tyrone, none of them is of any great height. At just over 2,200 feet, Mount Sawel has the distinction of being the highest peak in the Sperrins. It overlooks the beautiful Glenelly valley where the Glenelly River wends its way past Craignamaddy Mountain until it joins the Owenreagh River.

Mount Sawel overlooks Goles Forest, near the source of the Glenelly River. In this remote area, Goles Forest is an enchanting place in which to ramble or stop for a picnic. There is a small road that will lead you to the highest part of the forest. At the foot of Mt. Sawel is the tiny hamlet of Sperrin. The hamlet is an ideal starting point for anyone who wishes to climb to the summit of Mt. Sawel, but this is a venture only for the fittest. On a clear day the view from the top of Mt. Sawel is truly spell-binding: the River Foyle, Lough Neagh and the Mourne Mountains in Co. Down are all visible.

The Glenelly River, from its source, meanders down the valley past Mt. Sawel. The river is a magnet for fishermen for it is well stocked with fish, especially brown trout. Plumbridge, an attractive little village further downstream, is a popular rendezvous for anglers.

The Old Gate
DRAPERSTOWN

John B Haggan

Lough Fea is one of the delightful little lakes dotted throughout the Sperrin Mountain region. It is a long, narrow lake covering more than 100 acres and lies about five miles to the north west of Cookstown. To reach it from the town you travel up the Lissan Road through the Parish of Lissan towards Draperstown.

The word Lissan could be interpreted as the diminutive of 'lis', meaning 'little fort', but in this instance it means 'Aine's lis' or 'Aine's fort'. Aine was the fairy queen of the place and was guardian spirit of the O'Corra family.

Close to Lough Fea is Ballybriest Cairn, a very interesting archeological site. It is a double-horned cairn dating from about 3000 BC and was probably where cremated remains were interred.

The lough is in a very picturesque setting surrounded by a coniferous forest and heather-clad slopes. A path winds round it and there are good sites for picnics.

Lough Fea provides Cookstown with its water supply. However boating and canoeing are allowed on the lough which is also famed for its trout fishing. Mid-Ulster Angling Club holds the fishing rights for Lough Fea and anglers need a game fishing permit and a rod licence.

Many winters ago, during a prolonged period of hard frost, Lough Fea was covered with a thick sheet of ice. An intrepid motorist from the Cookstown locality drove across the lough over the ice in his car. Whether this remarkable feat should be regarded as a breathtaking act of bravado or an act of sheer lunacy is open to debate.

Mention has been made of Aine, the fairy queen. Continue on your journey from Lough Fea into the Sperrins and you are in true fairy country.

Lough Fea

John S Haggan

The People of Mid-Ulster

The O'Neills were one of the most prominent families in the history of Ireland. They could claim direct descent from Niall of the Nine Hostages who reigned at Tara from the middle of the 4th century. Some of his sons settled in Ulster and their descendants were the dominant force there from the 12th to the 16th century, known as Earls of Tyrone and Kings of Ulster. The word Ulster is derived from the Gaelic 'Ulidia' and initially the name denoted only the land east of the Bann, but gradually it came to mean the Ulster that we know today. The O'Neills were based in the area now known as Co. Tyrone. The name is derived from 'Tir Owen' - land of Owen. For centuries they were crowned in an elaborate ceremony at Tullyhogue, just to the south of Cookstown. The fort belonged to the O'Hagans, allies of the O'Neills, and they were responsible for the organisation of the coronation. Many of the O'Hagans are buried in the circular walled burial ground at Donaghrisk, close to the Tullyhogue fort.

The historian, J.A. Froude, provides us with an indication of the power of the O'Neills during the 16th century. Queen Elizabeth I decided that her Lord Lieutenant had not the capacity to govern Ireland in her name. Under new arrangements she decided that the north should be ruled, in the Queen's name, by Shane O'Neill who, in accordance with centuries-old tradition, had been crowned at Tullyhogue in 1559. Froude commented, "In O'Neill's country alone in Ireland were peasants prosperous or life and property safe." Shane O'Neill encouraged all kinds of animal husbandry and the growing of wheat.

He governed Ulster with a sort of rough justice and anyone who did not bow to his authority was dealt with in a summary manner. His position was that of an independent native prince. As he himself put it, "My ancestors were Kings of Ulster, and Ulster is mine, with the sword I have won it, and with the sword I shall keep it."

His sword proved useful to England in his expedition against the Scots who had come over from the islands of the Hebrides, arriving in great numbers and establishing a firm foothold. Shane attacked them, slaying their leader and this made him even more powerful.

O'Neill began to exceed the authority that had been agreed between him and Elizabeth and negotiations again took place. There was a meeting with Sir Thomas Cusack, the Queen's representative, in 1563 and Shane assured him that he had no intention of replacing the Queen's authority with his own. O'Neill even wrote an apology to the Queen and promised that in future he would be a true and faithful servant. Indentures were completed in which the Ulster Sovereignty was deputed to him in everything but name. By these articles, in consideration of him becoming a faithful subject, he was appointed Governor of Tyrone "in the same manner as other chiefs of the said nation called O'Neills had rightfully executed that office in the time of King Henry VIII". He was, "to enjoy and have the name and title of O'Neill with the service and homage of all the lords and captains and other nobles of the said people of O'Neill upon condition that he and his said nobles should truly and faithfully, from time to time serve Her Majesty, and where necessary wage war against all her enemies, as such manner as the Lord Lieutenant for the time being should direct." The Queen's letters patent, in confirmation of

these articles, expressed her entire approval of O'Neill's "present services", and the most favourable construction was taken of his former irregularities. This agreement with Shane O'Neill gave Queen Elizabeth's Lord Lieutenant, Sussex, an authority to deal with other disorders in Ireland.

O'Neill, however, still continued to drill and train his followers and increase his army, obviously in preparation for battle, and the Lord Lieutenant warned the Queen that O'Neill was planning to usurp her authority and was not satisfied with being a vassal. Elizabeth's reply was, "Be not dismayed. Tell my friends if he arises it will turn to their advantage; there will be estates for them who want, from me he must expect no further favours".

Shane did receive one more favour sent from Dublin. It was a gift of wine, on the orders, it is said, of Sussex, the Lord Lieutenant, but this was never proved. Shane was delighted to receive the wine and he shared it with guests, but the wine was poisoned and had almost fatal results for Shane and his companions. The circumstances surrounding this attempt on O'Neill's life were never made clear. However, it was discovered that the wine had been sent by Thomas Smith, a

Dublin merchant, and, significantly, Smith and the Lord Lieutenant were acquainted. Not unnaturally, O'Neill was incensed at this attempt on his life and insisted that the Queen have the matter thoroughly investigated to discover who was responsible for the plot against him. The Queen ordered Sir Thomas Cusack to instigate a thorough investigation to discover the culprit, whoever he might be. Thomas Smith was eventually arrested and at first he was adamant that he was innocent, but eventually said that he was responsible. He was later released, Cusack persuading Shane to forget about the matter.

In 1564 Sussex was removed from his position as Lord Lieutenant in Ireland. Owing to his lack of diplomacy, he continually stirred up trouble, making him unsuitable to hold office. He was replaced by Sir Henry Sidney.

As the years passed, Shane's influence had been steadily growing. He was, in effect, the undisputed ruler of Ulster but, although he could be extremely ruthless, O'Neill was a complex personality, and not entirely self-centred. Before meals he had food set aside for the poor for, as he said, "It is meet to serve Christ first"

O'Neill was not content with his lot and began

to expand his territory, much to the Queen's annoyance. The new Lord Deputy, Sir Henry Sidney, arrived in Dublin in 1565 and decided that Shane O'Neill would have to be curtailed. During a war of attrition waged by Sidney, O'Neill was gradually overcome and was left friendless. The clan leader sought sanctuary with Allaster MacDonald who had originally come from Scotland. There had been bitter differences between the two leaders in the past, so O'Neill's plight must have been desperate for him to have entrusted his safety to MacDonald. During the night, some of MacDonald's followers entered O'Neill's tent and assassinated him. It was an ignominious end for a man who had exercised such great influence and who had once been entertained at the court of Queen Elizabeth.

Hugh O'Neill succeeded his uncle Shane as Earl of Tyrone. He remained in favour with Queen Elizabeth until news reached her that he had harboured soldiers from the Spanish Armada which had failed in its invasion of England in 1588. The Spaniards had been cast ashore when their ship had foundered off the west coast of Ireland after their escape from the English fleet.

Differences began to grow between Sir Henry Bagenal, Marshall of Ireland, and Hugh O'Neill.

In accordance with custom, O'Neill had himself crowned at Tullyhogue Fort in 1595. He began to recruit widely over mid-Ulster and formed alliances with chiefs from Connaught and Leinster in preparation for the conflict. O'Neill obtained a quantity of lead which was supposed to be used for roofing his castle, but instead he had the lead melted down and made into bullets. Elizabeth had allowed Hugh O'Neill to keep a small standing army in the province. He constantly changed the recruits and by this method he gradually built up a large secret army which would be ready when required. In 1598 O'Neill's army met the English at the Battle of the Yellow Ford which was fought on marshy ground between the rivers Callan and Blackwater. O'Neill was victorious and inflicted heavy losses on the English forces with their leader, Bagenal, being killed.

Hugh O'Neill should now have been in an unassailable position as he was the uncrowned King of Ireland. However, his army was formed of irregulars and his men had to return to their farms and other duties.

In the meantime a new Deputy, Mountjoy, had been appointed and he was sent over from England to resume the war in Ulster. The Battle of Kinsale in 1601, despite Spanish assistance, was a setback for O'Neill. By pursuing a scorched earth policy Mountjoy wore down the Irish resistance and he ordered that the stone at Tullyhogue Fort, on which the O'Neills had been crowned for centuries, should be broken up. Although he had not actually been beaten in battle, Hugh O'Neill, realising the futility of prolonging the struggle, submitted to Mountjoy in 1603. O'Neill was pardoned and allowed to keep his title and most of his property but, in effect, the ascendancy of the O'Neills had ended in Tyrone. In 1607, realising that he was in a very vulnerable position and that plots were being hatched against him, Hugh O'Neill with the Earl of Tyrconnell and other chieftains sailed into exile from Lough Swilly to France. This came to be known as 'The Flight of the Earls'.

After the Flight of the Earls it was decided by James I that the time was ripe for the Plantation of Ulster. The plan was to divide up large areas of land in Ulster among Scottish and English settlers and various London Companies. The scheme of the plantation was the work of three commissions which sat between 1608 and 1610 and its chief architect was the Lord Deputy, Chichester. There were certain stipulations which the planters, or 'undertakers' as they were sometimes called, had to meet with regards to the property they had been granted. They were supposed to ensure that their property was adequately protected from the possibility of attack. Obviously some of them did not satisfy the agreement for Chichester complained bitterly in a communication, "They lye in weak thatched houses, and slenderly prepared for defence."

A house that met the criteria is Springhill, near Moneymore. It belonged to the plantation family, the Lenox-Conynghams, from Scotland, and is one of the handful of houses that replaced fortified castles to survive in its original state. The plan of the outbuildings with walled garden, warning bell and barn walls with gun slits indicate that the house was built with precautions taken to give it some measure of defence in the event of a surprise attack.

After the Cookstown Plantation there was a smouldering resentment among the native Irish and eventually an uprising was planned. It was hoped that the rebellion would be supported by exiles who had left the country after the Plantation and had gained military experience serving in continental armies. The rebellion was under the general command of Rory O'More, but the Ulster rebels were under the command of Sir

Phelim O'Neill, a nephew of the famous Hugh. Sir Phelim lived on his estate at Caledon which his father had been allowed to retain and, to all intents and purposes, gave the impression of being loyal to the Crown. He was given a knighthood and made a J.P. and in 1641, the year the rebellion erupted, he was even made an M.P.

Although Hugh O'Neill was the last of the clan to be honoured with a traditional coronation on the stone throne at Tullyhogue, Phelim O'Neill had himself crowned there, despite the fact that the coronation stone had been smashed by Mountjoy.

Sir Phelim initiated the rebellion in Ulster by making a surprise attack on Charlemont. During the course of the 1641 rebellion in which many lives were lost, there were appalling acts of brutality, accompanied by looting and destruction of property.

The rebellion was not having the desired success when Owen Roe O'Neill, also a nephew of Hugh, arrived from France. Phelim O'Neill handed over his command to Owen Roe and in 1646 this new leader encountered General Robert Munroe, leader of a Scottish army, near Benburb, between the rivers Oona and Blackwater. O'Neill scored a stunning victory. More than 3000 of General Munroe's men were killed whilst the Ulster rebels lost comparatively few men.

Cookstown suffered badly in the 1641 rebellion. There was an uprising in the vicinity led by Nial Oge O'Quin. He and his men took over the iron foundry of Sir Thomas Staples at Lissan and compelled the workers to make pikes and other weapons. The foundry was under rebel control for more than two years until it was later retaken by Royalist troops who went on a rampage and Cookstown, then merely a small village, was burnt to the ground.

Prior to this O'Quin had taken Lady Charity Staples to nearby Moneymore and imprisoned her in Moneymore Castle, though she was later freed. In 1642 Sir John Clotworthy recaptured the town which had suffered greatly at the hands of the rebels.

When Owen Roe O'Neill died, the rebellion was virtually over. Sir Phelim O'Neill had taken refuge on a crannog on Roughan Lough at Newmills not far from Cookstown. There are different stories related about his capture. One tells that his dog was heard barking while another goes that he was betrayed by a follower called O'Hugh.

Sir Phelim O'Neill was taken into custody by William Caulfield. He was taken to Dublin, found guilty of high treason, and executed in 1653.

The Siege of Derry figures prominently in Irish history and the Cookstown area has associations with it. William 'good Will' Conyngham, who built Springhill House near Moneymore, played a leading part in the siege, providing a regiment which he raised in his locality. He was later appointed a member of King William's Council of Six. A rector of Cookstown's Derryloran Parish Church was at the Siege of Derry, while another Tyrone clergyman, the Reverend George Walker of Donaghmore, played a more famous role in the siege as commander of the defenders at Derry. In 1690 he was killed, at the age of 72, at the Battle of the Boyne.

There is a well at Altmore, near Pomeroy, where King James stopped to water his horse on the long trek to the Siege of Derry. King William is said to have forded the Ballinderry River at Coagh on his way to the Boyne and at Cookstown he is supposed to have tethered his horse to the Drummond Oak whilst encamped nearby.

The 1798 rebellion arose out of the desire to

rectify social injustices and Presbyterian involvement was strong in Down and Armagh. There was not a general uprising in Co. Tyrone although the authorities, through their agents, were kept aware of the undercurrent of sympathy for the rebellion. A letter written by one Thomas Knox to George Lenox-Conyngham of Springhill in 1796 advised him that there was subversive activity in the neighbourhood of Coagh and asked him if he could find premises large enough to house 40 soldiers in the area. A pamphlet that came into the hands of the Lenox-Conynghams gave details of plans of County meetings of the United Irishmen. In the pamphlet they were advised "to abstain from spirituous liquors."

A member of the prominent Ledlie family was a captain in the United Irishmen. The Ledlies lived at Flood Lodge, near the confluence of the Ballinderry and Moneymore rivers. They owned a large farm and had a bleach green. Ledlie led a contingent to the Battle of Antrim in 1798 when the commander was Henry Joy McCracken from Belfast. At the outset the insurgents were almost victorious, but the tide turned against them and prospect of victory turned into defeat. Ledlie, fully aware that execution awaited him if captured, managed to escape. He eventually reached Cushendun where his only hope of survival was to flee the country. He took passage on the first boat that was available which was a fishing boat heading to Iceland. He eventually reached Canada where he made his home, and by all accounts did well.

Many other people who have left Tyrone to seek a better life on another continent have played a major part in a variety of spheres, including the army. Such a man was James Shields, who was born in Altmore, near Pomeroy. Shields became a close friend of Abraham Lincoln, one of America's most famous presidents, although on one occasion the fiery Shields challenged Lincoln to a duel. Shields became a general in the American Civil War and was the only commander to inflict a defeat on the formidable 'Stonewall' Jackson. He defeated Jackson at the Battle of Kernstown in Virginia, Shields fighting for the Union and Jackson for the Confederates. Shields also distinguished himself in the Mexican War of 1864.

Shields, a remarkable man, scaled the heights when he entered politics. He became Senator of Illinois and Governor of Oregon and he founded the town of Shieldsville, Minnesota. There are statues of him in the national capital, Washington; in the Minnesota state capital and in Carolltown, Minnesota, where he died. It is a strange coincidence that 'Stonewall' Jackson who opposed General Shields in the American Civil War had family roots not far from where Shields was born.

Those who can recall the Second World War and were there to witness the scene, will clearly remember the American soldiers arriving in Cookstown. Prior to that the only Americans whom people had seen were the heroes and heroines of the silver screen. The Saturday Matinee at the picture house in the Fairhill would have been packed to capacity with excited children who had paid their 6d to witness the daring exploits of their cowboy heroes Gene Autry, Roy Rogers and Hop-a-long Cassidy.

The first contingent of American soldiers based in the area, the 28th Quartermaster Regiment, arrived on the 16th October 1942. Watched by an entranced crowd, they paraded down the main street with the Stars and Stripes proudly flying. Besides being billeted around Cookstown, the American soldiers were based at Springhill, Moneymore. They also had an airfield at Cluntoe, Ardboe, where air crews received their training.

A recent article in the Cookstown History Journal referred to Private First Class Milburn Henke from Minnesota who was in 'B' Company 133rd Infantry. Milburn was the first American soldier down the gangplank when the Americans arrived at Dufferin Dock, Belfast during the war. The journal containing the article was sent to America and the recipient was able to contact Milburn's wife through the Internet. During the war years he had served in Egypt and received the Silver Star for rescuing a wounded colleague whilst under enemy fire. Milburn had been seriously injured when a lorry in which he was riding overturned, but he had made a good recovery and was promoted to sergeant before his demob. After the war his wife and he had returned to Northern Ireland several times and had been to Cookstown on one of their visits. They had planned another visit but sadly this was not to be. However his place is assured in the annals of military history as the first American soldier to set foot on European soil during the Second World War.

The war years also saw the arrival of other visitors who aroused considerable curiosity. No one in Cookstown expected to see German prisoners-of-war. They arrived by train and marched up the main street in their greatcoats under lightly armed guard. The prison camp, encircled by coils of barbed wire, was at the north end of the town, at Monrush, where there is now a housing estate.

Young boys brought cigarettes up to the prison camp and threw them over the wire enclosure in exchange for toys that the prisoners had made. The soldiers on duty up in their sentry boxes raised no objections to these transactions. The toys, carved from wood, were beautifully made and some had remarkably ingenious mechanisms. The prisoners had a football pitch in the camp and they were taken out from time to time to work in the nearby farms. In the camp they constructed a large replica of a Rhine castle out of stones and cement. When the camp was no longer in use the castle was carefully removed and has remained on display in private ownership.

* * * * * *

Much of the Cookstown area is rich farming land, so agriculture plays an important part in the economy. The town has three weekly livestock markets for cattle, sheep and pigs. The area has always been noted for the rearing of animals and of pigs in particular. In 1938 the ambitious decision was taken to build and equip a bacon factory, now called Unipork, on the outskirts of Cookstown, at a cost of some £50000 which was a considerable amount of money for the time. The factory was built adjoining the railway which was then in operation and a siding was run into the factory. The proximity of a railway line greatly streamlined transportation to other parts of Ireland and the U.K.

There have been several major extensions to the factory over the years and the number of employees has increased to about 400, making Unipork, Cookstown the largest employer in the area. Since the Second World War the factory has diversified from the production of bacon to include the manufacture of other pork products. In addition to their own brand items, the factory produces a range of products for multiples throughout the U.K. and even further afield.

Apart from the bacon factory, the area can also boast a cheese factory and a creamery. The Department of Agriculture has an agricultural and food technology college based at Loughry near Cookstown.

Fishing is of significant importance, both as recreation and as a source of employment. The River Ballinderry and its tributaries provide some of the best fishing in Ireland and this attracts anglers from other parts of the U.K., the Republic of Ireland and further afield.

Lough Neagh is teeming with fish. There are

many varieties to attract the angler, including trout, perch, rudd, salmon and the unique pollan and dollaghan. An important source of livelihood for lough shore people is eel fishing. This is an occupation that goes back into the mists of time, but the fishermen had a prolonged struggle with the authorities to gain the eel fishery rights. As far back as 1642 a fleet of Sir John Clotworthy engaged in a battle with a native Irish fleet. Following this encounter Clotworthy's successors, the Marquesses of Donegal, claimed the fishing rights of the lough. Eventually, in 1965, the Lough Neagh Fishermen's Co-operative was founded and acquired a 20% share in Toome Eel Fishery. The Co-operative obtained complete share holding in that company in 1972 and, with it, ownership and control of eel fishing rights in Lough Neagh. The lough shore eel fishermen are based mainly at Kinturk, Aneetermore, Ardboe and Lower Back.

The life cycle of the European eel is a fascinating story. Born in the Sargasso Sea in the North Atlantic Ocean, the eels are spawned at a great depth and, on surfacing, the larvae are carried eastwards by the Gulf Stream. After three years they reach the Lower Bann and enter it on their journey to Lough Neagh. When the elvers reach the Salmon Leap on the Lower Bann they encounter elver 'ladders', made of straw ropes, placed there by the Toome Eel Fishery Company. The elvers climb these 'ladders' to reach the higher sections of the river where they enter tanks and are transported by lorry to be released into Lough Neagh. Some 20000000 elvers are released into the lough each year. If the elvers were not transported it would take them three years to reach the lough. They would reach it in a weakened state and be simple prey for pike and other large fish.

In the lough they feed and grow for about ten years and at this stage are known as 'brown eels'. They are caught from boats using long lines. The lines can be four to five miles long and have up to 800 hooks on them baited with worms, small perch or pieces of pollan fish. When the eels are ten years old, they become 'silver eels' and head out of the lough down the Bann for the Sargasso Sea to spawn and die. Silver eels are caught in nets in the Bann by Toome Eel Fishery at various weirs.

Most of the eels are exported to the continent, although a sizeable proportion goes to the Billingsgate Market in London. The eels are carefully stored and are transported live or frozen to their destination. Lough Neagh is Europe's largest source of eels.

In earlier times an important source of livelihood for the people of Cookstown and district was found in the various processes of linen manufacture. Up to the middle of the 19th century the work connected with the production of linen was a cottage industry, the spinning and weaving being carried out by small farmers who then brought their product into the nearest market to be sold. At the market, flax seed would be sold to the farmers to produce their next crop of flax.

Rough linen had to be beetled and then bleached to give it its smooth, white finish. The more well-off bleachers employed agents to buy the linen for bleaching at the various markets. These agents were renowned for their endurance and would often ride as far as thirty miles to a market.

By the mid-1850s the linen industry had ceased to be cottage-based and, in the Cookstown district, had moved mainly to various localities along the River Ballinderry as far as Coagh, using water power to drive the machinery. Families connected with linen manufacture in Cookstown were the Adairs, Gunnings and Leepers and, in Coagh, the Duffs.

When production was at its height as many as 1000 people were employed in the linen industry in Cookstown.

The Cookstown area is rich in natural resources and this has been of great benefit to the town and its locality. Its considerable number of quarries have produced sand and gravel for the building trade for many years. The presence of an ample supply of limestone and shale near the town was instrumental in attracting the Blue Circle Cement Company which started operating near the Sandholes Road in 1968. The plant can produce 50% of Northern Ireland's total cement requirements. It has a workforce of more than 100 and there is enough raw material available to keep the plant in production well into next century.

In the mid 1800s the roads to and from Cookstown were no more than primitive tracks. This was confirmed by the comments of John Wesley, the founder of Methodism, who travelled by horse on his preaching missions and stayed at the Grapes Inn in Milburn Street, Cookstown.

The planning and making of roads presented considerable difficulty. The native Irish did not take too kindly to the construction of roads as they viewed them as a danger to their security. They could see that, with the improvement of lines of communication, the authorities would be in a better position to act against them. The difficulty of laying down roads was summed up by the comment that it was "as dangerous for Englishmen to attempt a general survey as to take arms in a general conquest, the Gaelic people having been as hostile to a map-maker as a soldier, for to their minds the appearance of either surely portended confiscation."

However, long-distance travel on horseback or by jaunting car was replaced with the stage coach. Travelling by stage coach, especially for the outside passengers, was cold and comfortless, and there was always the danger of being waylaid by robbers.

With the arrival of the train in Cookstown, transport was revolutionised. It greatly improved trade as Cookstown now had an efficient way of transporting livestock and agricultural produce. The trains also provided the people with a convenient way to travel.

When trains began operating in Ireland in the early 1840s dire consequences were foreseen. It was predicted that the smoke would kill the birds, cows would be terrified into witholding their milk and horses would become extinct as they would

not be needed. There was also serious concern that houses with thatched roofs would be set alight by the sparks from the trains. Passengers travelled first, second or third class. In early third class travel the discomfort endured by passengers was horrendous. The carriages were open at the sides and had no roofs or seats. The passengers were simply crammed in, standing upright.

The railway station was constructed at Molesworth Street and had two railway companies using different sides of the station. The London Midland and Scottish Railway began operating in 1856 and the Great Northern Railway in 1879. The passenger services ended in 1956 and many people still have fond memories of travelling by train on seaside excursions to such places as Portrush and Bundoran.

Nowadays, Cookstown is easily accessed from all directions and is convenient to the M1 and M2 which provide direct routes between the area and the main customers of its various industries. Cookstown has proved to be an extremely suitable place to set up business due to its central location; a ready workforce; generous government grants and a forward-looking District Council. Many industries are situated at the Derryloran and Ballyreagh Industrial Sites, while Cookstown

Enterprise Centre provides work and office units as well as excellent conference facilities. Apart from Unipork and the Blue Circle Cement Company, important employers in the area are Keystone Lintels and the American company, Copelands, which has recently set up in the town.

* * * * * *

Cookstown has excellent facilities for a wide range of sports. Recreational provisions include water sports at Ballyronan Marina, a splendid leisure centre with its swimming pool and Killymoon golf course, as well as facilities for football, hockey, bowls and tennis.

Golf has been played on the Killymoon course for more than 100 years. Socially, Killymoon Golf Club has had an important role to play in the town for, over the years, all creeds and classes have worked closely together to make the course one of the finest in the country. The club, set in splendid surroundings near Killymoon Castle, was founded in 1889, the first captain being Hugh Adair of the linen firm. His daughter Rhona was the finest player that the club has produced. Her achievements in the world of golf were remarkable. She won the Irish Ladies' Golf Championship four times and was twice winner of the British Ladies'

Open Golf Title. One leading golf journal of the time was ecstatic in praise of Rhona Adair, declaring that she was the greatest lady golfer in the world. Once, in 1903, when she arrived back in Cookstown on the train after one of her victories, she was given a rapturous reception by the town. Seated in the family carriage and preceded by two bands, Rhona was hauled in triumph by the local football team all the way from the station to the family residence at Glenavon.

A highlight of the town's year is the annual Cookstown 100 Motor Cycle Race. Founded in the 1920s, the 'Cookstown 100' is a popular event for motor cycle enthusiasts. During the war years the race was not held so the first race after the war, in 1946, was keenly anticipated. The town was thronged with spectators lining the race course which, at that time, included the long main street. As the race is run on a handicap system, the results could not be immediately declared once the riders had crossed the finishing line. It took the officials a considerable time to work out the placings but, at last, the winner was announced. It was a local rider, Geordie Reid, riding a Velocette. The jubilation of the crowd was unbounded.

Cookstown has many attractions for the visitor

with its shops, sporting facilities and excellent hotels and restaurants. It attracts many shoppers and has a splendid weekly market, held on a Saturday. The town is situated in almost the exact centre of Northern Ireland, surrounded by an area that is renowned for its unspoilt, varied scenery. To the west are the rolling Sperrin Mountains with their many scenic, recreational and archaeo-logical attractions and to the east is the vast expanse of Lough Neagh whose shores are steeped in history.

There are many places of interest to visit, such as Killymoon Castle and Tullyhogue Fort and numerous archaeological sites including the Beaghmore Stone Circles. Ardboe Celtic Cross compares with any High Cross in Ireland. Two interesting National Trust properties are the 17th century plantation house at Springhill and Wellbrook Beetling Mill which is a fascinating reminder of the linen industry that once thrived in the district.

Nearby are Drum Manor, Davagh and Gortin Forest Parks. At Ardboe on the lough shore is Kinturk Cultural Centre, where the visitor can learn about aspects of Lough Neagh and its environment.

* * * * * *

People who emigrated from Ulster to America may have left their country but they took their culture with them. An example of this is a folk song called 'The Streets of Laredo' which was made popular when recorded by the well-known American folk singer, Burl Ives. The melody is the same as that sung to the familiar local song 'The Bard of Armagh'. The bard of Armagh was Phelim Brady whose real name was Dr. Patrick Donnelly, Bishop of Dromore. When there were restrictions on freedom of religion, he tended to his people by travelling among them disguised as a minstrel called Phelim Brady. Dr. Donnelly is buried at Desertcreat, his birth place. When he died he was brought there by his faithful followers, travelling at night, staying at houses along the way.

Tyrone has its own bard, William F. Marshall, known as 'The Bard of Tyrone'. He was born in Co. Tyrone in Drumragh in 1888, his father being the principal of Sixmilecross National School. He graduated from the Presbyterian College, Belfast and later came to his home congregation where he was installed as minister in 1916.

His poems are an evocation of the rural Co. Tyrone that he knew and loved so well. He had an acute ear for the Tyrone dialect and his humorous poems are masterpieces that are a wittily observed but never unkindly reflection of the lives of the people he knew intimately. Not all his poems are humorous and his more serious poems can stir up genuine emotion. W.F., as he was called by his friends, was keen on angling and on his fishing forays he came to know every nook and cranny of his parish. He was at one with nature and his poems about its hills, valleys and streams capture the very essence of 'Tyrone among the Bushes.'

A nature walk has been developed called 'The Marshall Trail' so that people can visit the places that inspired this local poet. If you read his poem that so wonderfully evokes the mystery and solitude of Bernish Glen and decide to go there, you might be disappointed if you do not sense the presence of the fairies.

The Arts are still important in Cookstown today. A prime example of the town's forward-looking spirit is the new Arts Centre, in Burn Road, built on the site of the former town hall. The Centre has a multi-purpose auditorium which can seat 350 people or provide standing space for more than 600. The tourist information centre, formerly at Molesworth Street, has been relocated to the foyer of the Arts Centre. The

Centre has a civic reception suite and a retail outlet selling locally produced arts and crafts. There is an exhibition and workshop area and refreshments are available at the cafe. The Council intends that the Arts Centre should provide a wealth of entertainment. Shows and events to suit all age groups and tastes are planned, including musicals, concerts, drama, pantomime, etc. The local community is encouraged to express what it would like to see in this new centre. Space can also be hired by local groups and organisations wishing to promote their own events. The Centre is community based and community owned and provides a valuable focus for the Arts within the Cookstown and mid-Ulster District.

*   *   *   *   *   *

The Cookstown district today has a population of about 32000 with Cookstown itself containing more than 13000 inhabitants.

At the beginning of the 1600s the town of Cookstown was, literally, not on the map. Where Cookstown is today there was only a rough track running through a wilderness, part of the immense forest of Glenconkeyne. The track connected various religious establishments sited at places such as Ardboe, on Lough Neagh's shore, and Tullyhogue in the south of the area. A clue to the existence of religious establishments in the area is the fact that near Cookstown is the townland of Grange which generally means 'monastic granary'.

Cookstown owes its foundation to the Plantation of Ulster in 1609 which began after the Flight of the Earls in 1607. Settlers from Scotland and England were encouraged to come over to Ulster by being given grants of land to develop. One of the 'undertakers', as they were sometimes called, was Dr. Allen Cooke. Cooke was the founder of Cookstown and established the beginnings of the town in the 1620s. An English ecclesiastical lawyer and a Master of Chancery, Allen Cooke was a distinguished scholar. The territory in which the construction of Cookstown commenced was known as Mallenagh and was owned by the O'Mellans, a family of the Erenagh, one of the ancient Irish tribes. They were responsible for taking care of travellers and providing for the bishop on his visits to the district. In their charge was St. Patrick's Bell which is now housed in the National Museum in Dublin.

In 1622 Cooke obtained a lease from the Archbishop of Armagh of land that was then known as Corcreighe. That area would today lie between Coolreaghs, to the north of Cookstown, and Burn Road which joins the main street from the west. There is no sign of a burn there now, but it does exist. It was culverted under the road many years ago.

There were certain stipulations connected with these grants that had to be met by the lessee to ensure that the land would be put to good use. For instance he had to build a house that would be "fit for an Englishman to live in." One can only conjecture about what would then have been considered a suitable Irishman's dwelling. Cooke, although he did not live on his property, did take his responsibilities seriously and constructed ten houses at 'Old Town'. This part of the town retains the name Oldtown and Oldtown Hill is a famous landmark. Oldtown has changed since those times but unchanged, looking north, is the stupendous view of Slieve Gallion in the Sperrin Mountains. Slieve Gallion means 'Callan's mountain'.

In 1628 Cooke was granted a charter by Charles I to hold weekly markets and twice-yearly fairs at what was known as 'Cooke's Town'. The markets were very successful and this was underlined at the indictment of the Earl of Stafford who became Deputy of Ireland in 1633. At his trial he was accused of conduct that had destroyed the markets of many of the towns in Ireland. Mention was made of the fact that, because of the regulations that Stafford had introduced, the trade at the market in 'Dr. Cooke's Town' which had raised the excellent sum of £100 per week, had been completely undermined. The goods on sale at the market: grain, flax and linen, both finished and unbleached, give an indication of the economy of the area at the time.

Just off the top of the Loy Hill, running west, is the Fairhill Road. It is so named because in former times this is where the farmers drove their cattle in from the countryside to haggle over prices. It has long since been replaced by a modern livestock salesyard off the main street. The twice-yearly fairs held in Cooke's time are thought to have been held in an area north of Oldtown. The weekly market has always been held in the main street of the town.

During the 1641 rebellion Royalist troops burned the town to the ground in their conflict with a rebel leader, Nial Oge O'Quin. For some years after that the town was in a sorry plight with only a handful of inhabitants living in mud and thatched cottages. However by 1646 there were enough Scottish settlers to merit the founding of a Presbyterian Meeting House at the 'Old Town'.

The lease of the town was acquired in 1666 by James Stewart. The Stewarts were the foremost family in the district, having acquired considerable grants of land in the district under the plantation scheme. In 1671 Stewart built a castle on his demesne at Killymoon, just south of the town near the Ballinderry River.

In the 1830s, William Stewart, who had inherited Killymoon, decided to build a new town in the grand manner stretching south from 'Cooke's Town'. John Nash, who designed London's Regent Street and Brighton's celebrated Pavilion, was given the contract for laying out the town. Stewart's plan was remarkable and unique to the country. Cookstown has a main street that is more than a mile long and 130 feet wide at its broadest point, making it the town with the longest and widest main street in Ireland. It was intended that every main street house should have a rear garden of about 100 yards long and, indeed, due to Stewart's foresight, nearly all the houses were provided with a garden of that size.

The long main street of Cookstown has many changes of name which is confusing for the stranger. Starting from the north there is Milburn Street, named after the nearby linen mill. Waterloo Place in Milburn Street and Waterloo

Terrace in the adjoining Moneymore Road were named in memory of a local man, Ensign Lynd, who worked on the Killymoon Estate. He enlisted in the army and distinguished himself at the Battle of Waterloo in 1815 as a member of the locally-raised 95th Foot Regiment. This regiment later received a commendation from Wellington, which was a great achievement as the 'Iron Duke' was not a man to lavish praise where it had not been earned

In Milburn Street is the Grapes Inn, originally a thatched, two storey building. Built in 1752, it was Cookstown's oldest original building remaining practically unchanged until it had to be rebuilt in the 1960s. Moving south, there is Oldtown Street, then William Street, named after King William and James Street, commemorating King James. In James Street there is the imposing First Presbyterian Church, constructed in 1840.

Loy Street, means 'street with the hill'. In Loy Street, replacing an earlier building, is the impressive Roman Catholic Church of the Holy Trinity, consecrated in 1860 by Cardinal Dixon. Adjoining it is the chapel of St. Brigid's Convent designed by Laurence McConville and completed in 1965. The Methodist Church in Loy Street was built in 1858 having been moved from its original

site. In Church Street is Derryloran (St. Luran's) Parish Church designed by John Nash in 1822. It was rebuilt in 1861 but retained the Nash tower. Next is Killymoon Street, then the Linen Hill which was named after the nearby Adair's linen factory. This area is known locally as Gortalowry which means 'O'Lavery's Hill'. From the Linen Hill, the road leads over the King's Bridge which is recognised as the southern entrance to the town.

In the centre of the town is Molesworth Street which leads east off the south end of William Street. Molesworth Street is named after Viscount Molesworth's daughter, the mother of William Stewart of Killymoon who planned the town. An attractive feature of the street is the railway station building which was retained after the trains stopped running and, until recently housed the Tourist Information office

Armorial Bearings

The Town Commissioners used to meet at Molesworth Street before they were succeeded by the Town Council whose offices are now on an elevated site at the bottom of the Burn Road.

Cookstown District Council was formed in 1973 when Cookstown Urban and Rural Councils were incorporated into one body to administer Cookstown and its district, following the reorganisation of local government. The Armorial Bearings of the town were adopted from the Coat of Arms of the former Urban District Council which had been granted in 1969.

The Armorial Bearings is a striking insignia incorporating in its design features that graphically illustrate the dominant characteristics of the town and area and the factors crucial to its development into the thriving community that it is today.

On top of the crest is a Phoenix, that mythical bird, which was consumed in flames only to rise, rejuvenated, from the ashes. During the 1641 rebellion, in a confrontation between insurgents and Royalist troops, the few houses that then comprised Cookstown were burnt to the ground. But, just like the Phoenix, the town rose again.

The cog-wheel on the shield symbolises industry and specifically the linen industry which provided employment and played such an important part in the economic growth of the town.

The sheaves of corn on a green background illustrate the importance of agriculture to the Cookstown district and are also a reminder of the very progressive agricultural college on the out-skirts of the town, at Loughry.

Killymoon Castle features on the insignia. Rebuilt in its present form by William Stewart in 1802, it is a well-known landmark in the town and features prominently in its history.

The colour blue on the crest represents Lough Neagh, the largest inland lake in Great Britain and Ireland, which forms the eastern boundary of Cookstown District. Its importance as a fishing area is incalculable and its unspoilt shore is a haven for plants, birds and other wildlife. The area adjoining the lough is rich in history and his-torical relics and it is a compelling attraction for local people and tourists alike.

Included on the crest's design is the Red Hand of Ulster. The red hand was also part of the emblem of the O'Neills, Earls of Tyrone and Kings of Ulster who had a close association with Cookstown area for many centuries.

The motto on Cookstown's crest is 'Forward' and, given the progress that the town has made in the past and the exciting plans that there are for the town's future development, it is an entirely apt description of the dynamic spirit that motivates its people.

Sources

L.I. Byrne, Irish Kings & High Kings, England.

B. Messenger, Picking up the Linen Threads, Belfast, 1988.

M. Elliott, Wolfe Tone, London, 1989.

M. Scott, Irish Myths & Legends, London, 1992.

E.M. Patterson, G.N.R. of Ireland, England, 1962.

J.K. Charlesworth, Historical Geology of Ireland, 1963.

"Look Back", Mid-Ulster History Journal, various editions.

The Mid-Ulster Mail, various editions.

S. Lewis, Topographical Dictionary of Ireland, Vol. I, Dublin, 1837.

C. Russell, The Crisis of Parliament, England, 1971.

A. Day & P. McWilliams, Memoirs of Ireland, Ordnance Survey, Belfast, 1990.

M. Lenox-Conyngham, An Old Ulster House, Ireland, 1946.

Lord Macaulay, History of England, England, reprinted 1967.

P. Loughrey, The People of Ireland, Belfast, 1988.

Northern Ireland Poets (anthology), 1995

Dear Reader

We hope you have enjoyed this book. It is one of a range of illustrated titles which we publish. Other areas currently featured include:–

Cottage
Publications

Strangford Shores	Donegal Highlands
Dundalk & North Louth	Drogheda & the Boyne Valley
Armagh	The Mournes
Belfast	Fermanagh
Antrim, town & country	

Also available in our 'Illustrated History & Companion Range' are:-

Ballycastle and the Heart of the Glens	Larne and the Road to the Glens
Coleraine and the Causeway Coast	City of Derry
Hillsborough	Banbridge
Ballymoney	Holywood
Lisburn	

We can also supply prints, individually signed by the artist, of the paintings featured in the above titles as well as many other areas of Ireland.

For more details on these superb publications and to view samples of the paintings they contain, you can visit our web site at **www.cottage-publications.com** or alternatively you can contact us as follows:-

Telephone: (028) 9188 8033   Fax: (028) 9188 8063

or write to:-

Cottage Publications
15 Ballyhay Road
Donaghadee, Co. Down
N. Ireland, BT21 0NG